Civilian

Deonte Osayande

Crossroads Poetry Series
Three Fires Confederacy
Waawiiyaatanong ✦ Windsor, ON

First Edition. February 2019

Library and Archives Canada Cataloguing in Publication

Osayande, Deonte, author.
        Civilian / Deonte Osayande.

Series statement: Crossroads poetry series |

Poems.

Canadiana 20190059656 | ISBN 9781988214269 (softcover)

Subjects:
        LCSH: Osayande, Deonte—Poetry.

LCC PS3615.S26 C58 2019 | DDC 811/.6—dc23

Book cover design: D.A. Lockhart
Cover Image: Deonte Osayande
Book layout: D.A. Lockhart

Published in the United States of America and Canada by

 Urban Farmhouse Press
www.urbanfarmhousepress.com

The Crossroads Poetry Series is a line of books that showcases established and emerging poetic voices from across North America. The books in this series represent what the editors at UFP believe to be some of the strongest voices in both American and Canadian poetics.

Printed in Chaparral Pro

*Dedicated to Damani "Kash" Marlin, Chantay "Legacy" Leonard,
and David Blair*

Contents

Cardiac

Post Credit Scene: Fireworks /3
Microaggressions /5
Mavis /6
Old Times /7
Lazarus /9
Whale /10
Expendable /12
Awkward /13
November Nights /14

Cost

Cost of Growing Up /19
Clouds /20
Making the Statue of Liberty Vanish /22
Enchantment /23
Devils /25
Scarecrow /26

Cracked .

The Cracked Out Russian Stripper /29
Being Helped Out By Another Uber Driver /31
The Uber Driver Speaks /33
In the Kitchen /35
4 East /37
President Citrus /39

Cinematic

Star Wars /43
V for Vendetta/Fight Club /44

Children of Men/Seeking a Friend /46
for the End of the World
Eternal Sunshine of the Spotless Mind /47
Jurassic Park /48
Plot Twist /51

Capitalism

River /57
Pussy /58
Neanderthal /60
Life Lessons /61
Monsters /62
Zombies/Resurrection /63
Going Home /65
When a Poet Dies /68
Things We Carry With Us /69
Capitalism /70
Thirsty /72
Cooking Rice /73

Casualties

Dreams /77
Disrespect /78
Porn /79
Casualties /81
L'appel du vide (Drawn to the void) /82
Hungry For Desire /84
This Loneliness Kills/Therapy /85
Skin Doesn't Know Your Touch /88
Pet /90
Body Count /93

Criminal

Arrest /99
Humility /101

Dehumanizing /102
Cattle /103
Prisoner /104
Non-consensual /106
Sleeping in the Cell /107
Gender /108
Why Don't You Call Me /109
Dear Jon /113

Connection
Litter Box /117
Connection /118
Death by Cop /121
These White Men are Dangerous /123
Innocence /125
Blackness /127
The Plague /129
Mental Straitjacket /131
Mausoleum /134
Teachers /136
Blood /146

Chronology
Poem Texted to Myself in the Bed /151
Tiny Prayers /152
Gushers /153
Soundtrack /154
Prison of the Mind /155
Alternate Realities /156
What Was Left at 18063 Woodingham /158
What Happened at 15791 Cherrylawn /160
Smudged Glasses /161
Strange Witchcraft /162
Hanging in There /163
The Cycle /164

Mistaken For Monsters /166
Lycanthrope /167
Feet /168
Conversations With My Past Self /169
African Dolls /170
Lessons /171
Blame /172
Calamity /174

Acknowledgements /177

About the Author /179

Cardiac

Post Credit Scene, Fireworks

My car, their chariot
through the night
as they watched
the lavender explosions

burst into the night. Their father
irritably listening to every comment
they made, every remark about

the fireworks. I'm thinking
isn't this too blackness? To be

enjoying something as simple
as these three little boys
watching the fireworks
with their dad in the back seat

of my car, while I am just the uber
driver trying to get from one destination

(engaged) to the next (marriage). My fiancee
asks me to stop driving, and although we need
the money to pay for the wedding I comply

because we need to spend as much time together
as possible. Last week police killed two people
for nothing but their blackness and I see why
the father of these boys sat in my car as red
with irritation as could be. He wanted to get

home. I want to get home. Home, where
my fiancee can cry in my arms until her eyes

turn purple. I make them light up, exploding
when I enter the room. Like a firework. That too
is a blackness, to be the life of the party every time

because there is no life without you. There is no
culture without you. They can kill our bodies
from now until the cows come home but then

Microaggressions

To be told you're so articulate, to hear
how smart you are as if you're not
supposed to be, to be told what you are

despite your opinion, to hear a welcome
to the performance poetry world instead
of just the poetry world, to be told how

you're rare to have come from your
environment as if that is a compliment,

to hear how you're a tiger, endangered
all the time, when you just want to be,

to feel the impact of microaggressions
when nobody else can feel them so they
don't believe you about your tragic pains.

Mavis

2001, skies have not yet fallen,
looking her up, years later,

shocked to discover
fiction, based off of

Haitian women,
and isn't that black,

image stolen and you don't get a dime
from the very thing you are famous for.

2017, and ebony women
still stolen treasures, still

missing, unreported,
after emancipation,

wondering how much black blood
should be shed before white people

stop drowning Atlantis,
in the failed design

of their flirtations. Caught
in the Bermuda Triangle,

filling machines with water, then
complaining about their aqueducts

Old Times

Why did I begin
to like cheese is
a question that is too
easy for me to answer.

Your fried chicken tasted
of ninety six, good times,
gym shorts and Sega Genesis,

my shoes all drawn on and my mom
in the kitchen. It takes me back

to a simpler time, mac & cheese, chicken
and greens, not a care in the world, I was
carefree. No zealots or bigots. No terrorists
or 9/11 or fear, just a young boy, his dinner

getting cold and sonic the hedgehog. Gotta
go faster was his catchphrase but I wish
I could have taken it and rushed back

to these peaceful moments of the past.
Asking me why I'm so fond of these

times, I try to tell myself
he's a good guy. Growing
up together, played on the same

basketball courts with one another
but I can't shake the badge, the uniform,
the betrayal, how someday I might just be
another black life to him on the other side

of the gun and he might remember
reasons to punish you. What happens
when that becomes him? When the gun

is pointed at him and he doesn't have
enough time to pull out his badge
or show his ID. I wonder if black lives

will matter to him then, calling them
rowdy kids looking for something
to protest. protesters don't riot

when murderers die.

Lazarus

My body rejects attempts to drink milk, so
I guess I struggle swallowing white lies. Being

black in a black city ruled by white profits,
there is a fear of our sharpness, our words, fear
of biting the hands that feed us as if these

same hands haven't been force feeding poisonous
political policies to the people, targeted zombies

unless we make the agenda easier to consume. We
get extracted and exterminated, unless we make
the rebirth look pretty enough to produce more prophets
willing to move in. Detroit isn't making a comeback. That

would mean it would have to die first. Schools get
closed. We go bankrupt after hosting every major sports
championship. Water gets shut off after the mayor can

somehow find funds for new stadiums, and a train. Not
much is known about the life of Lazarus after his rebirth.

Nobody to locate him. No body to locate when the missing
person is forgotten. Everyone praises the resurrection
without remembering the other Lazarus, how he was left to die.

Whale

Amnesia kicks in
trying to bring up
my first time riding a bus,
the motorized whale. Every

window, a blowhole
where I could see

how cold Michigan winters
can be. My sister and I left
from the bus stop around
the corner and then I remembered
this isn't about the first time

when my eyes gazed onto the passing
scenery but it's about how I first found

myself on the track, how I originally
was trying out for the basketball team
because niggas don't try out for track

without some origin story in football
or basketball or some other sport
that only track can condition you for. Tryouts

begat an offer instead, a thought
which was beached, on the bus

ride to our first track meet I thought
how did I end up here. All of us
wanted to be athletes since it was
what we were taught boys like us did

but we were never given any idea
of what was out there besides
shooting or throwing a ball...

...or dying.

Expendable

In sports, everyone
eventually becomes replaceable, the lucky
don't see who's next biting at their heels

and in the end our bodies are on borrowed time,
eventually betraying us, with loan payments

that we have to pay later on in life
but I always knew I was expendable
from the day my high school coach
told me he never favored me and tried

to have me replaced by a runner who
wasn't even as fast as me and one
that I thought was my enemy

until we had guns drawn on us
when we returned to school.

Awkward

Walking in on your coach
getting replaced is like
accidentally stumbling
into your parents having
an argument about affairs
that happened years ago
or walking in on your brother
masturbating or maybe before
all of my memories crumble
around me I should just stop
stumbling into rooms unannounced.

November Nights

You don't know love until you've had
your lover hunched over, drunk
throwing up all over your bed sheets,
blanket, comforter, sweatpants, hoodie,

and whatever else she can find. It's orange vomit
all over your things and you're busy trying to figure
out if that's a pineapple chunk or orange slice? Anyway,

you don't think about how disgusting it is, or how your
whole room will smell like barf for the next week, all
you're thinking about is how you have to hold back
her hair as she pukes her lungs out because you love her

and she loves her weave and you can't let anything
happen to it, and besides, she does look good in it. I mean
if you can't love someone at their sloppy drunken pants off,
dance off, one second and throwing up while crying,

and peeing the next worse then you shouldn't love them
at their best. Honestly, you have to love her through
the smelly farts and snotty noses and she gets to love you

through sickness and in health, whether it's a electrical
charger through your foot or just a cold. It's a two way street,
and it isn't easy. Love each other equally and totally, through
everything and back. A time will come when you will need

her and she will be there. Cussing you out for being so ill
or injured, but there nevertheless. Caring for you as you did

for her in her time of need. So, go ahead, scoop up her puke. Shit, if you need to put it in a zip locked bag and roll around in it. I don't know why you would need to do that, but I do know the sense connected to memory the most is smell and you don't wanna ever forget the smell

of that mess. Show her the humor in it, that you two have been through worse and made it out the other side. Embrace her, because you two have lovedeachothertrulythroughitall. What'sonedrunkennighttoalifetime?

Cost

Cost of Growing Up

Watching movies on the bus
between track meets, the distraction
helps me forget how much work I need
to put in to keep this scholarship. The cost

between track meets, I need the distraction
not to think about this. The effort I have
to put in to keep this scholarship. The cost
of quality education anchors me, but we're

not supposed to think about this. The effort
needed to learn, survive, adapt, evolve. So much
for quality education anchoring me, weighing
down our bodies. The bus hugs each curve

to learn, survive, adapt, evolve, like our bodies
over time changing. Now, I need to learn how not to
down our bodies when depressed. Buses hug each curve,
keeping us from descending over the guardrail

of time changing. Now, I need to learn how to just
watch movies on this bus. Not thinking so much about
my body descending over this guardrail we call age,
how those thoughts help me forget how much work

goes into gradually growing up in America.

Clouds

forecast for a rainy day
filled with wallowing,

depression, exactly as
meteorologists predicted,

radar system focused
on the funnel clouds

forming over
your mood.

thunderstorms rolling in,
lightning strikes until

there is nothing left
of the joyous little boy

you used to be
your agony spread out

across a lifespan, that is
too long to go on. You think

about the sun, how your mom
can become like that, rising again

from parasitic, the cancer,
how it will rise with her,

it grows like your regret
of mortality wasted,

all the instances where
we smiled and laughed,

shared mother and son moments.
When they cut all of it out,

the damage
already done.

Making the Statue of Liberty Vanish

fables grew larger
until the guilt grows,

crushing me under it's weight,
buried underneath, self doubt,

second guessing while
making rabbits appear

out of a hat.

my downfall, my design,
innocent intentions handcuffed

to me, the art of being confined
pleases me. I know the things

I care for our safe,
all the memories,
all the photos,

haunting me when I'm locked away. so
so when you ask why I didn't look in my wallet
when preparing to get my ID for this hotel room
with a woman who is not my ex-fiance, debris
left over from the man I was before I vanished

Enchantment

All the items were placed around the fire
as the spell was prepared. Ready to water
everything with my tears, primed to plant
ingredients all over, I was starting to wind
as the spell was prepared. Ready for time
to play it's part in this magic trick, ground

ingredients all over, my body, laying on the ground.
To play it's part in this magic trick, the fire
had to play it's part in this magic trick and it was time
for it all to be consumed by the refreshing water.
To play a part in this magic trick, before the wind
blew ingredients all over my body and these plants.

For it all to be consumed by the newly refreshed plants
they all had to be sacrificed to the earth, the ground.
Ingredients, all over my body, ready to be one with the wind
in this moment. Everything is consumed by the fire,
they all had to be sacrificed to the oceans, seas and the water
and it was a beautiful thing to witness it happening in real time.

In this moment everything is consumed by time,
even the other versions of ourselves we try to plant
and it was beautiful to witness all of the falling water
filling all the holes, graves, blanketing the hollow ground,
even the other versions of ourselves tried to fire
us from this job that had to be done. Evidence cast to the wind,

filling all the holes, our graves, gifts given to the wind,
and as the moments pass alternate versions of us pass to time.
From this job that had to be done, evidence cast to the fire.
With them go memories that the alternate versions of me plant

and as the moments pass the alternate versions of us go in the ground,
    devoured by the bottomless lakes, seas, oceans and all the waters.

With them go memories of the alternate dimensions, the face water
    all of it vanishing, mementos lost to blow off into the wind.
    Devoured by the endless graves, limitless tombs, and the ground
all the items were placed in six distinct spots, like a clock telling time,
vanishing, mementos caught in the underbrush and the living plants.
Everything with my tears, the memories, this spell, gone with the fire

Devils

Happy people don't interfere with the happiness of others, welcom-
ing this devil into out lives years before, not knowing what I was
doing. One date would dissolve everything I desired, two years later,
the secrets came to the light. Regrets fall like snow blanketing every-
thing dreamed of, meanwhile she gets to laugh at her nefarious deeds.
Drinking with no guilty conscience, sleeping fine at night, whereas
I can't slumber without having terrors at night anymore, without
thinking of what could have been, should have told my partner about
her, how vengeful she is, how jealous she would be about our engage-
ment, how I dated Lucifer, but this Satan didn't matter. Now, in the
basement of Hades, sitting thinking about my oversight, my regrets
become pains that are supposed to happen, punishment for past deeds
forgotten about. Fitting that a poet would destroy everything my life
was supposed to be. Living a work of fiction wasn't supposed to be my
life but in the end it all ended as a pipe dream, fantasies I couldn't live
up to. Faking it until making it. This wordsmith of lesser moral stan-
dards threw me into the depths, and here at the bottom fighting a tug
of war between myself and what is right.

Scarecrow

Paused at different intervals
when hearing the specter

of her voice call out a score
for a poet in the poetry slam

grief, the fickle creature,
the straw coming out of clothes

no longer worn. Shame in the mirror,
this ghost of a man standing in your

reflection. Trying to imitate you,
even though they say it is the highest

form of flattery, it isn't when he's trying
to force you out into the field to deal with

what you have been avoiding

Cracked

The Cracked Out Russian Stripper

Accent thick molasses, pouring
out of her, asking to be taken

to her apartment downtown,
above this bar where we had held

open mic nights years before,
reminded me of this Polish woman

I was friends with years before,
couldn't swallow the thickness

of what she was saying. Years later,
kisses on the cheek for friendship,

but today, she is married,
and I am swallowing my dignity,

like glasses lumpy, frothy,
white milk. Didn't even realize

they said it in my car, slipped out
and isn't that how racism always is?

slipping out,
not meant,

given with some
weak ass apology?

the way he kept calling me his boy,
his fiancee apologized for hearing it too.

I heard nigger, each time,
the racism, America's tit,

oozing with breast milk
forced down my throat

and I'm sick of seeing this utter stuttered
out again, and my memories of passengers

past are all blending together, some
white concoction, and we're finally here

Being Helped Out By Another Uber Driver

Midnight, frosty rain falling down
on your uncovered head, struggling
to get the lug nuts off because you

weren't given the part to remove them much like how
in high school someone passed a secret
Valentine's Day card to you with the name
of the sender not filled out but suddenly

without asking, a stranger pulls up
to offer help and it reminds you of

the time you drove a passenger to the ER
while he was talking about unicorns
and black holes, and the other topics that

come up in his dreams since speaking
in his sleep is something he inherited
from his father, and you know this
because in trying to keep him awake

due to his blood loss in the backseat
but you're telling the other fellow

about this because in talking with him
you both confess to be Uber drivers
and he talks about a time when he was
in need of help and nobody stopped

on the side of the road to help him
so he couldn't leave someone else

suffering the same fate as he did and isn't it a blessing
to bond with a stranger over no reason other than
needing help on the side of the road and someone
comes to your rescue to help you out while your passenger

walks home in the dark unknown.

The Uber Driver Speaks

On the way to high school track meets
boys and girls who were dating stuck together.

my first year back riding the bus,
the joy of being cuddled up,
cherished time because we knew
it wouldn't last forever.

retelling this story to a passenger in my car
and they ask what happened to her, if we saw
happily ever after together and I don't know how

to crush all of her hopes for a happy ending, for
the conclusion where she goes off to college
in Florida, leaves me behind
gets happily married to someone else.

stall until we reach the airport and she leaves me
as well, another person entering my life

and I'm telling them another story, this time
about my first time drinking, how it was
in college, saying nothing, just grabbing
what I had seen destroy so many others,

a flood of car crashes
all happening at once. contents
expelling out of me in a sludge

of sunflower seeds, alcohol, and secrets,
this broken water main, leaking too much
from my lips, eroding bridges between people.

I told them that now, seven years later.

my doctor said I have enlarged neck muscles
from holding in the things I don't say

and isn't it odd how the universe works
in mysterious ways, how
tested we become.
isn't that a miracle?

how we aren't some accidental hit and run,
left to bleed out on the street, someone's child,

lost long ago,
body never found

In the Kitchen

I've learned how to cook various
side dishes since you've been gone,

got how to cook ground beef,
chicken and chili. I put all

the ingredients in, mix them
together but it isn't the same

as learning recipes from your
grandmother. I'm sorry I didn't

think to learn from you then. I know
it's too late now, can never taste

your cooking again but at the very least
trying is something I'm willing to do. I know

every time the light flickers in the bathroom
that's you, busting in on me one more time. When

I buy those oatmeal cookies that you used to like
one of them mysteriously goes missing, every time.

five years and I still miss you. I've lost more people than I can count
with my fingers and I just want those moments back. I don't

want to remember you carted off on a stretcher, I want to
recall the way you used to always say fridgedare instead

of refrigerator. I don't want to remember
final breaths on that bed in the backroom, I want

to remember the time she called my dad, her son, a good
for nothing nigga and he didn't say a word. I don't want

to remember Chantay in that hospital room, I want to recall
all the times we laughed together while taking care of her

cats. I guess what I'm saying is, the afterlife must not be
that great if you're still lingering around here. I feel those breaths

on my shoulders when I'm in the kitchen cooking, subtle
reminders to include little hints of ingredients and I guess I just

want to know that you're alright. I want to know if there is an
afterlife, after life, after all, because I don't believe anymore

4 East

On the day that I killed myself
I went to sleep and woke up
The following morning.

I drove here, where
We haunt the hallway,

Walking back and forth,
Ghosts that have lost
There way. In death

I found therapy, found sleep,
Found medication which

Helped me. I saw a bird
At my window and thought
Of you, thought of my cat,
The memories we shared.

There is no pain in death,
But there is pain in knowing

You hurt your loved ones. I've said
My sorrys so much they've become
Cliches, water thrown about

And having no impact. I fucked up,
Told lies and ended up in this

Purgatory in the process. Even still,
Despite all I've done, you still visited
Me in this afterlife where I became

A shell of what I once was. All the bills,

All the money, doesn't matter here
In the psych ward. What matters

Is what you can do for the people
Who matter when you become a shadow
Of what you once were. There's this saying,

If you hold a bird too tight it will struggle
And then die, but if you let it free it might

Come back to you, it might not,
But you can enjoy hearing it sing.
I was so scared of losing the ones
I love that I silenced their songs. Now,

I let them go, and it hurts but I need to
For my own resurrection. I need to so

I can some back to life, stop being
The undead zombie I was when I tried
To do everything to please everybody

But myself. I'm ready to go into the light
And enjoy millions of tomorrows, thousands

Of times I will smile and hundreds of times
I will laugh. I'm ready to go now, to live
My life to the fullest.

President Citrus

President pumpkin patch kills me with
his policies, old blonde dead pigeons on his head,
looking boy, claims he can tell me about my healthcare.

Meanwhile, under his reign, my life, a war torn nation,
suicidal thoughts whirling dervish in my head. On the day
I was conned out of my engagement ring, a year after I had
proposed, my favorite rock star gave his life to the same beast

stalking me. Rich and famous, depression doesn't care,
causes supernovas of sadness inside us all. I almost followed

if it weren't for president cantaloupe, cradling the country,
crushing our hopes and dreams. I can't go out now, not while
this demon destroys democracy, and isn't that what depression is,
evil spirits in our brain, touting the terrible times while ignoring all the
good

graces we've been granted. Only dead things don't evolve, grow and change
and my life is in a constant painful state of flux, but it should be. In this hurricane
finding rays of sunshine, another lover who accepts all of my flaws, who pillow

talks about fighting president peaches. But even if I hadn't found this
I would still have so much to live for. Bring it on president creamsicle,
with your

tiny hands for your tinier thoughts. With your safety vests
of deceit. President citrus, I'm gonna resist you until the day
your carrot face is no longer in office. I'm combating you

with the same intensity that I'm fighting these illnesses in my brain with,
which is to say you're going to need more than a few traffic cones

to stop the resistance, President goldfish, you and depression
are going to need to more than that.

Cinematic

at the end of the day
all of the galactic
plunder, oppression,
entire planets being
destroyed, severing
of limbs, so many
deaths, were all
for the chance
at eliminating
the emperor
and to share
quality time
with his son,
rule over the galaxy
as father and son,
a family held together

as one, with the force

Star Wars

I.

order or else,

we all fall to chaos,
they don't understand

that, even

if you don't like it, there
is no security without

rules, without ruling
parties to keep some
form of order, even if

it's horrifying, together

II.

without a little anarchy
in our lives, following
orders until our eventual
slaughter, what would we be.

you made me after all
and I made you
the bad ass who you are

today and this is how
you repay me. Your

little imaginary friend?
People always using you,
us, until they get what
they want but I would

never think you would do that
to me, to yourself, to both of us,

until death do we part

V for Vendetta/Fight Club

and the fate of the world
lies in a black woman's arms,
again. After fifteen years

of no children the first one,
born with this woman

traveling with a suspected terrorist
because anyone not bending to the will
of our overlords must be a terrorist, right?
And isn't that sad, our greatest love stories

always end in tragedy. Love, another form
of death, the old you evaporates for another,

the end of what you were
before, but what would I know
about love? just a hunk
of space rock hurtling through

space. I have known gravity
after all, how it compels you
to be with another being

to the point of destruction. You
were just some girl, on a hunk
of rock floating through space,
having no significance to my life,
the villains, are always the heroes

of their story.

Children of Men/Seeking a Friend for the End of the World

We never went through
this horrible breakup,
I just mysteriously
got a cat all by myself.

We never were engaged,
arguing new years night.

Never got a house together,
went to New Orleans together,
saw those movies with each
other. You were never in
the hospital with me lying

by your side. You never
got drunk and threw up,
we never even went to

that open mic together.
You were just some girl.

Eternal Sunshine of the Spotless Mind

I.

we were weapons, beasts
created for your own

entertainment. you caged us
knowing our instincts would
kick in. we're not from this time

period, so of course falling back
on what we know, what we were

bred to be. you're always making
monsters and then shocked when
they don't want to bow down
to their architects. the funny thing

about Frankenstein, how the name
of the scientist becomes associated
with the monster, as if the scientist

wasn't always the monster all along.

II.

They were fossils,
constantly buried,
below times long
ago. They were
endangered, not
supposed to be
alive, in the white
mans world, but
they are still living,

defying all expectations
for us. They keep dying,

all the time, not by
asteroids, global
warming, or any other
machines of the universe

but by you, and us,
as designed by you,

to be surpassed by
you, and isn't that
the most difficult,

when what is supposed
to be extinct, refuses
to finally die the original
man, back again for revenge,

by everlasting life. He asks
"did you say the white mans
world?" and I apologize for

my inaccurate portrayal
of the exhibit he's observing.

Jurassic Park

I.

always scared of the clan,
so much so that he would
have never suspected

the police to do him in. He called
them to help with an attempted
robbery at his home but now,
he's laying in a pool of his own
blood, not knowing it was them

all along. Months prior, He dreamed
of traveling to Africa. Never in his
wildest dreams would he imagine

he would be shot because they got
the wrong address on an African
suspect in the sex trade. Once
released from the hospital,

he went to the basketball court
and next thing he knows he's wet

on the floor and wondering
whether that loud noise
he heard was a car backfiring
or a gunshot into his body.

He wakes up, traumatized
from his experience
with the cops. Tries to take a ride
in his car to relax his nerves and
as he's driving through an unfamiliar
hood he notices all the people standing

on the street looking at his car. He's suspicious
of them but he doesn't know their afraid
of the creature on the roof of his vehicle.

Stopping at a movie theater
to see a new film, he noticed
how it was a packed house. After
the movie ended he left, looking

back to see which theater he went to
and shockingly it was the same closed
cinema, boarded up and abandoned

forty years prior. Sitting there,
his clothes, tattered from tear
and wear all of these years,
homeless, squatting, and just

getting over the hallucinations
all he wanted was a simple life,
simple desires and I am just

the writer, imagining
all of his great tales

II.

escaping
in film,
the cinema,
ends with us
coming back
to a reality
we didn't choose.

distractions
only lasts so long,
movie reels,
memories,
all deleted scenes
on the editors floor,

in front of the big
screen. Pretending
to be someone else,
actors portray others

for applause, for awards.

meanwhile the atrocities
going on
right outside
of their windows

Plot Twist

Capitalism

only a few blocks away
as kids. our families
close. our fathers

friends to this day.
Playing together,

in the street. fighting
from time to time, as boys do

but always coming back around,
being friends again. talking,

school,
sports,
girls,

giving advice. Once invited
on a double date by the river

and although it didn't work
out, just the gesture

was nice enough for me. didn't know
years later, this very fresh water,

taken away from us, left
unless we paid prices

that those who had money
would not have to purchase.

River

cats meow
for
communication
with humans,
not with
each other,

but my kitten
doesn't,
and who am I
to tell him
he is wrong,

that I'm not
a being who

requires
food,
water,
affection,

that I don't need
to be constantly
checked on, made
sure I didn't execute
my own self on what
I hunger for, for what

I crave, and when he
licks my face I know
that at least someone

appreciates
my care,

another

day, another nurse
I fall in love with
because I need
healing, another

heartbreak
and maybe
that's part
of the process

Pussy

older. same
college,
in the heart
of the hood.

both staying
in dorms
away from family

which only stayed
blocks away. looking

out for one another
until one night, one
party, one two many
drinks. and here lies

another man, trying
to impress his friends

and my hands
are the weapons,
guilty of using.

Neanderthal

wings on your back,
cliché tattoos, taboos

to fill flesh with feelings
everyone has. similarities
ending, differences in
growth. grades may suffer

but the lessons must
be learned. become
scarred tissue without

the skin to match,
everything unseen.

the damage you show
will reveal all others
need to know about you.

I told one of my best friends
how I wanted a tattoo
of wings on my back
and he got it. I told

the same comrade
about a woman.
he dated her.

now, we no longer talk.

Life Lessons

"It's so nice
to see
someone

as young as you,
reading a book"

she said, not
knowing that
I'm an author
and for once

it felt comforting
for the monster
of fame to not

follow me
into this
bookstore,
to be another

nobody
looking

for something
or nothing
as all, because

fame is that wish
you should have
never asked for,
you might get it.

Monsters

guilt from the church,
the inescapable
feeling, fleeing
captivity from
it all, blame
for being human,
natural urges,
disguised sin,
temptations
of flesh
instinctively
bred in us
like animals,
suppressed
emotions,
when wicked
payments
promise
peace
from
poverty,
megachurches
built underneath
crosses can't
blanket the sick
and starved
while preaching
about coming
Armageddon
and salvation,
when for many
the end of days
we'd welcome
never comes
just more fees
for the wealthy,
as we starve
because we

don't eat them,
metaphorically
speaking

Zombies/Resurrection

they told me
to go back home

but this country
is the only
place leaving
the lights on
for me. I knew

what they meant
although they didn't,

how can a black person
return to Africa when
they don't know
where they are from,

but I do. again, this
the only home I have,
and it's funny, how
they don't realize
that love and hate
are relatives, living

within the same homeland.
to hate something, you have
to care about it, rather it is

indifference that is the true evil
shadow haunting us all. they

are so concerned about this house,
they spew out hateful phrases
at the residents they share it with,

the immigrants,
poor, minorities,
disabled, if we

weren't here
to do the chores
you don't want
then surely this
house would be
in disarray. loving

people who don't
share it back
has become a favorite
pastime of mine

but it is when
after the nights

we spent together
under the stars
speaking about
our dreams,
aspirations,

and I finally
don't remember
your name,

to be forgotten
in the history
books, not even
footnotes
left over
that truly
stings you. When

returning
back home,
here, I will not
glorify the names

of all those

who hate me

for the color of my skin,
because I don't know them
enough to care about their
issues and problems with me

Going Home

oceans of words
dry up, leaving

us barren of
moments we
can share with

you. And it happens
year in, and year out

against our will
for we can't stop
death, we can
only hope to be

immortalized
by what we say
before our time

is up, and we
join that great
list of names
for those who

passed
before

When a Poet Dies

registration,
proof of insurance
and my id. debit

card. The many
nights spent
with lovers
who were not

my other half.
memorized poems

and the half birthed
ideas of others. cell
phone for writing

those concepts down,
and for texts and calls

but I don't really speak
to anyone. your voice,
and times that we laughed
together,moments we

shared and the image
of your face before
we had to bury you

Things We Carry With Us

basic training.
finishing college.

two different kinds
of classes, struggling

for water, the both
of us, on separate

battlefields. deprived
of food and water

except financial struggles
are grenades for me. for him

the bombs are more literal,
his body covered in shrapnel,

my pockets as empty as his ammo
out in the field. this shared battle

we tried confronting
from opposing corners

of the globe. our shared
adversary commanding

our actions. this game
of chess, for resources

they all control.

Capitalism

tainted water
insures
the deaths

of many of those
looking to grow,

but what happens
when we do not
die, the lead
used to kill us

but now it builds
bulletproof resolve,

mutant skin because
rather than spend
money fixing issues

officials treat themselves
to nights on the town

in new stadiums built
off the backs of our kids
since their schools

happened to be closed,
and understaffed but

what would I know?
just a guy currently
in love with a woman

cheating on me
though I don't know
from this city,

Thirsty

united in need
of decent water

simple.
just pour
the package

into the bowl,
add water and
stir. but my nerves,
those roads during

earthquakes, anxiety,
checking every couple

of seconds. the fear
of something going
wrong and then
the whole apartment
engulfed in flames

and there is no way
out. Sweat rains
from your pores,

pouring out of your hands
trying to hold on to spatulas
which you have never touched
before. All this time you're

spending concerned about
what can go wrong, you

didn't even notice, your meal
which you are so worried
you can't eat it, is done.

Cooking Rice

Casualties

Family, sitting
together around
the dinner table

as the father joins
hands with his wife

and daughter in prayer
before the child proceeds
to pass the mashed
potatoes to her brother

who just a moment ago,
was feeding the dog

as they all happily
enjoyed each others
company and I, well

I am a bystander, envious,
jealous, for what I can't have
inside of this house, staring
into their living room window

wishing one day my dreams
will finally come to be realized.

Dreams

to travel
across
oceans

to video blog
the forest
where many
have taken
final breaths
at their own

hands, stating

the body
you found
after
laughing,
nervously,

wasn't your
intent, apologies,
not accepted,

how inhumane
one must be to
consider
others
like gruesome
attractions

for your filmed
entertainment

Disrespect

watching videos
of black couples
together before

sex, not wanting
to forget what
it's like, having
love, blizzards
surrounding

as this lack
of affection
continues,

honestly
the fault
goes
where.

this
curse,

to want
embraces,
harvests

during drought
takes over
my life. all I want,

feeling connected
to someone
but I've grown
so much   so detached

from everything
that I don't even
recognize the man

in the mirror. blessing
or not,the flesh aches
for another, whose
face I can imagine

Porn

intersections await. thinking,
about just letting the car go
where it pleases, terrible wrecks,
your fossilized body among

the items found. or better yet
you can make sure there are no

other casualties of your mistakes,
off a bridge, into a river, to the depths
with you for one last time. You

consider it, the light turns green,
your ex is still happy, and you
are still miserable, but you continue

to drive home, because this is your life
now. moving from one light to the next,
there are red times, yellow times, and green,
but your life continues, the beast doesn't win.

Casualties

chemical composition causing
sleep in me, everyday bear,

hibernation. call me a dreamer
some bound to be nightmares.

drawn to the void, thinking
about drifting off to eternal
darkness, car coasting off

the side of the road, or lying down
in front of it as it rolls over me,

not taking my medicine because
the risk of getting sick and dying
in this ditch on the side
of the freeway watching the cars

drift by into the evening night
deja vu takes hold, the day
all of my friends and I went

outside to play, for the last time
although we didn't know it, this
curse inside of me, drawing
me to the back of my eyelids

for the last time. she said
to love someone, you
have to know how

you would kill them,
which I thought
was odd, until
I found out
that she
would have
convinced me

to do it for her

L'appel du vide (Drawn to the void)

midnight shadows.
lady of the night
fleeting quickly,

leaving after loving,
this silent betrayal.

only one of my kind,
searching the internet
for others with this
name. silence,
unbearable.

at times
alone,
at parties,
alone,
concerts,

always wanting
time with myself,

by myself

craving the noise
of your wetness
meeting mine. feeling

the flesh of you.
delicate flavors,

famine sweeps the land
where I walk. remember
starving of your scent.
malnutrition,

I've hungered
for too long
to stop now.

Hungry for Desire

months earlier
after talking
to the universe

about collecting
his roommates
piss, I decided
that this person

right here, crazy.
needs to be
in here, but what

of me?
mood
shifts.
needing

antidepressants,

this
life
jacket
keeping
Mr Hyde
at bay,

now. this

drowning,
overwhelming
waves
of emotions.

anxiously
floating

above the surface,

taking on water,
wanting wellness.

to be not haunted
by the ghost ships
in my brain. recalling
times when failing
my loved ones.

months ago,
to be like him
six years old
in a seventy
year old body.
presently

prescribed
lifeguard
in a bottle,
repeatedly

for the moments
sanity submerges
me under the water.

she

teasing about my depression,
about my anxiety, about
my bipolar. lovers laughed
at moments when turmoil
was too emotional/mental

she

scoffed at me,
witnessing
breakdowns,
hospital visits.

she

who had full knowledge
of what she was doing,

keeping my pains
chained to this
sinking ship.

she

told me handle my problems
like a man,
bury it in cigarettes,
or alcohol, so I could
get back to work, get back
to taking care of her.

This Loneliness Kills/Therapy

wardrobe, now filled
with clothes I don't
wear, skin takes
about one month,

I gave it nine.

made sure
my blood
cells would
have enough
time, in case

you tried
crawling
back to me.

touching
my flesh,
seeing
what
became
from your
betrayal,

my hair,
a field
growing

from
seeds
you had
sown,

it is so wild
now, enjoying
the journey
taken

without
your words
anymore

Skin Doesn't Know Your Touch

I want that type of love
you can't talk about
in public spaces.

Embrace my funky,when
I walk through the door,

I miss feeling intimate
inappropriate cuddles,

I wanna hug you while
you are taking a piss.

Romance my toes
when they are tired.
The floor isn't lava,
my feet are, lay with them.

Linger in my lap, look up at me
lovingly, and just lick my face.

Be the one who can make
my bear hugs bearable,
baby hibernate with me.

Be my little strawberry,
my snicker doodle,
my sour patch kid,
first be sour, as long
as you're sweet after.

Risk it all for me
try my cooking
knowing dang well
I can't cook but
let me sustain your life
longer with my love.

I know depression is a dragon,
laying it's heavy weight on me,
smoldering the ground where
I step. I know the bitter taste

it leaves in your mouth,
embraces my self destructive
thoughts when it shouldn't,
going kamikaze on those I hold

close. Social media cries for
help reek of neglectful silence,

and if it wasn't
for the last one
to love me for me
I wouldn't be here

today. What I'm saying is,
his name is Dwayne.
He's black. We've known

each other for about a year
and we give each other that
unapologetic, absolute kind
of love and you gotta do

better than that, better
than my cat to capture
my heart. He licks

my fingers,
lays on my chest,
all big eyed
and lovingly. just

stares into my pupils.
rest your sweet head
on my books,

not for knowledge
but because you know
how important they are

to me. it is said
that elephants
have great memories
and react to people
the same way people
react to puppies

can you find me cute
in that same innocent way?

Pet

Slept with my fair share of monsters
but haven't asked one
about their body count

since my first one, and can barely
remember if it was in the silence
of dorm room walls
which never tell
or in the basement

of my parents home
where I got tricked
out of it by someone
who wanted another
notch in their belt,
not knowing how it felt

to be the hunter
for once. We're
all terrible

when the lights go out
and we become people
who take or want to be
taken instead of cared for,
and I don't know if the child
of the one that made me a ghost

haunting their marriage
is mine but I do know
one thing, that karma
is someone standing

opposite your six shooter
with a machine gun. I guess
I mean to say don't be a taker,
I guess what I mean to say
is don't be one who enjoys

being taken from. I guess

what I mean to say is I have
a problem separating love
from just sex, and I may not

have been as passionate
but I also didn't know how
to love every last one of them,

from the poet who left me,
to the poet who we kept secret,
the affairs that we're acted against
me and the ones I brought on myself,

these are not just bodies to me. I give
each and every one a piece of my soul,

and do you know how terrible that is,
to have your mind wandering
for four different lovers
in four different states,
in one week, to care
about children who wouldn't recognize
your face if they saw you today

because you once loved their mother,
to wonder if they are still alive today
or rotting underneath somebody's

body count? I have loved and let go
far more than I would like
to admit, and it is more than what
the eyes can see, the skin can feel,

the handcuffs around my being
keep my memories attached

to each and every person. The ones

who have swallowed me whole
and the ones whose flesh I've
coated, and all that lies
in between. I have loved them

all and I can't stop loving them,
even if my adoration changes,
so don't ask yours about body counts

ask if they know how to love
for one night or for forever.

You don't want this curse,
to have given your heart
to so many, that you don't
even know if it is yours anymore.

Body Counts

Criminal

above cities
of salt, with

busted eyeballs,
eyebrows, arms,
and tailbones

my car, with all
of these injuries

is pulled over,
since quotas
are a thing
which cops
have to get
enough of, and

because it has
these injuries
sustained over

one winter
because
the roads

and their craters
had to make my
vehicle a victim
alongside others

around it since
the governor
couldn't be
bothered to put

down the salt
to melt the ice

on the streets
that we live on
and that is reason
enough for me
to be behind
bars speaking
to you right now

Arrest

until being taught
by this room, with

ten men and three
toilets, no stalls

just our bare backsides
behind bars, underneath

blankets which we were
issued. Poop will stink,

comes from all of our
bodies, whether it comes

out the butt, or out of
the lies that we tell.

Before, you could
sneak away from

it, who smelt it
dealt it, but now

everyone in the room
knows it was you, so

own it. Everybody
poops, don't be

ashamed, we all
make mistakes

and have to clean up
after those lies we told.

Humility

sharing
satire,
stories,
sleeping
space,

and slop
we had
to eat,

these
artificial
foods
made
of nothing,

becoming
makeshift
family in
county jail.

in here
when
thanking
the guards
for horrible
meals served

they were shocked,
having forgotten
all along, that we
are humans after all

Dehumanizing

our nation,
on the verge
of war, rumors
spreading

like a plague,
that if troops
got here
no matter
the charge

they would
have to
execute
all of is

inmates
for fear
of threats,
like cattle
when it
can't be used

Cattle

originally, thoughts
entered my mind
that nobody would
find me desirable,
the curled dreadlocks
on my head wouldn't

find hands willing
to massage my scalp,
these full lips, never

able to kiss another
again, delicate hands
would forever lack
another body to stroke
comfortably as we

lay lovingly together.
I am my mothers son,

which is to say,
I have known
love like eggs
to be crafted
with gentle
brushstrokes.

some would say
I'm too feminine
but all I desire

is desire, all I want is
to be wanted, not rules

based on gender, no
games to be played
because of the vines
between my legs. All

I want is a woman
to love me for me

and my everlasting
beauty, and who
would guess that
I discovered how
handsome I am in jail

Prisoner

A guard
saying
it's not
like
the movies

explains
nothing
to me, to

someone
realizing

the same
thing
everyone
in here fears,
some people

have to go home
to every night

Non-consensual

happiness, for them
even if I have to view it
from secret accounts

social media
the cancer where we all must
live with our lonely

sleeping on this hard
floor, imagining her face
across from my own

instead, greeted by
another man, dreaming of
his own paradise

Sleeping in the Cell

when raised
to not know

how to cook,
or the difference
between

dolls and action figures.
To be restrained by these
concepts, and ideals
everyone adheres to, notions
which you never consented

to. When your mom knew
deep down, craving another

daughter, but got you
instead, still brought
you up with as much
love as she could,

the woman in a man's body.
You know you would have
still been persecuted, for

being black, or woman,
so you stayed man, but
then you would have
turned out a lesbian

so no matter what
you are an other.

Gender

behind bars
with nothing
but time, trying

to reach out to
anyone on
the outside,
nothing felt

lonelier

than calling,
dialing their
number and

getting
no answer back
except for
the void,
it's haunting voice

echoing back at you,
telling you to succumb
to the illness in you,

that there is
no gawd

in here
for you,
and when
you're at
your bleakest
moment

of depressions
darkness, you

finally get an answer
from your mom,
remembering
all the times
you forgot
to call her
when you got home

Why Don't You Call Me

I.

graduation,
grad school,

siblings
growing,

missing
you. I
wondered

what you
were up to

but I was told
in the time
you were gone

you started anew
in Florida, wife
and child I never
got to meet, whole

different person,
starting over. Looking

at your younger brother
and seeing your face,

reliving all the moments
shared, memories, times

when thinking I knew you
because we came from
the same streets but I didn't.

II.

so much has
changed now
that I don't know
where to start

this. I finished
my degree
and even got

another one. When
seeing your younger

brother, I can only
see you, and I weep
silently to myself
some nights. Your

baby sister is so big
now, I wish you got
a chance to see them

both. Your dad, well,
he's been broken
ever since we found
out, but your mom,
I don't know what
she thinks. She's
never come around

so I guess some things
never change. I saw

photos of your daughter
when she was a baby
but she must have
grown up to be so

brilliant. I wish

I could go down
to meet her, but
that would be weird

wouldn't it. Also
wishing I could
have met her
mother, remember
we had always talked
about the women

who we would marry. Now,
my ex fiancee broke up with me

and even still I'm wondering,
as brokenhearted as I am
what she could have done
to fuel enough rage to kill.
I guess I will never know.'

Dear Jon

Connection

cleaning my trunk,
this was waiting

to be scrubbed and moved
into my home
beside my bedside

because it's my
best friend's litter box,
because the cancer
took her away too soon.

can't return it, so I keep it
where nothing shits on

our relationship,
all the good advice
shared, and now

my cat just took a dump
in it when I wasn't looking

Litter Box

every time
having one

remembering
my grandmas
voice, sweet
tender, memories

gone from times
long ago, still,

my mother,
her daughter,

can't enjoy these
same delights
since her surgery,

the cancerous
intestines
gone, from her
body, habits
which grew

into illnesses
she stays
faithful to
like a church

feeding you
nothing
except
traditions
causing
diseases

but they comfort
you, until your
last days, when

you are sharing
silent moments

with descendants,
eating cookies
in the solace
of your old room

Oatmeal Cookies
solemn peace
achieved.
constant
ringing
stops. bills

paper for debt
collectors birthing
daily, checking
checking account

daily, trusting banks,
loving snakes
not expecting
bites. daily
stress. silenced,

killing your grief
eating orange slices,
citrus pleasure
flows from your mouth.

nobody looks for you,
unanswered calls, texts
go unread. This wanting

to be connected
all the time, scary.
to be
easily
found.

everyone
wants to be
famous. until
they are.
everything
accessible
at our fingertips. once
I wanted it, once
I ran, found it,
the speed
online,
results
breathtaking...until
there are no more breaths
to be consumed left.

Connection

I.

entire small town
exterminated
by some foreign
power.

      call it genocide,
            intervene.

but on our own soil
we hold rallies
in support
of the murders.
exclaim

you need to hear them
out, not all of them are murderers,

they just stand by
      it
          while the others
commit crimes.

remember the number, recall
every name as you try to
drink your morning coffee.

II.

minutes
choking
him out,

officers
decorated
in blame
in they eyes
of the public,

protests and marches
for justice, dwindling
until nobody cares
except one person,

his daughter
left standing,
left fighting
after all this,

left fighting
for her life,

heart attacks
from the stress
of keeping
her fathers memory
alive, until

she can't breathe
anymore

Death by Cop

A play in three parts

///

scene

teaching class to mostly white kids,
two voices in the hallway refer
to the lunch server as this nigga,

asking my students about safety,
the foreign concept to me, while
they're reading a story about
tired homeless men beaten
and imprisoned by cops.

Safety speaks mandarin to black America,
shootings become mass, growing in size,

churches become places where we sing
to a god who will not come, unless for
the gunman, with pure white snow for skin.

scene

in my youth I had nightmares of burning
under the hands of white blood cell hate
groups. Fearing I would be killed by these
terrorist cells, I would get up to get a drink,

noticing how the news would show these
victims to violence who always looked
like me. These people were never described
as people, never protected by the NRA,

see now, why the black boy has nightmares, you
can't spell slaughter without laughter, the Klu Klux Klan

are comedians, the joke's punchline keeps repeating itself
like history and we never get to learn it, if it's really funny.

scene

Searching my glove compartment
for registration, proof of insurance,
voices over my shoulder, officers

screaming curse words like bullets from the guns
of the dozen of squad cars around my one hundred
and fifty pound frame, you could see why anyone
would be afraid, of this nightmare scenario.

End Scene

these white men are dangerous.

toxic white masculinity, a nightmare
we can't wake up from, stereotypes
they're convinced are hiding underneath
their safety blankets made of guns, when
the monsters are in their own heads.

The lone wolves kill in masses justified
by the single instances when the killer
is a person of color retaliating against them.

this history of national domestic violence, we
point fingers at the world without mentioning
that this is the only place this happens. Imperialists
institute institutions for imaginary freedoms threatened,

it's in our history as much as the blood circulating in our veins,
the punchline, how the most privileged people are the threats.

These White Men Are Dangerous

is a hot dog a sandwich?
are koalas bears?

because I voted for Obama
the second time am I
complicit in the bombings?

all cops
choose
their jobs
over our lives

right?

the fear
instilled
for what?

hypothetical protection?

the first death
on their watch
and another, and
another, and another, and...

oppressors operating openly.
dancing with the very children
they shoot. playing basketball,
asked to stop killing us,
answer, nah. offering
ice cream cone, but asked
to stop deportation to nations

bombed, nah. why go to college
if the conclusion is death

by empire anyway? Are

koalas bears? They tell us
not to worry about it, as if
they can't still maul us anyway

Innocence

I.

newborn,
belonging
to someone
else,
hold it,
feed it,
dance,
sing,
rap,
play,

eventually,
eat it, or
return it
for killing,
for erasure
of the fact
that you
ever even
embraced it

II.

majority black city,
rampant poverty,
the new train runs
across the length
of downtown,

the only area
majority white.

sure, just coincidences.
white supremacists
get restaurants
in the new arena,

where people of color
held back from protesting
by the police
but allowed to spend
money while the establishment

talks about how they're animals. sure
it's just coincidences, all of them.

Blackness

Everyone asks is Detroit
getting better, and I answer.

What planet are you
White people from?

It's getting better, for white supremacists,
like the state, like the country. Downtown
Detroit is so whitewashed you can taste
the bleach in the air. Invited themselves

to the cookout, when they don't
know anybody there. Our melanin
absorbs the same things as plants
but you, it burns, so again I ask

what planet are you from? Because
this whole solar system been ours.

Jupiter has a huge hurricane on it's surface,
but have you heard of Irma, Sandy, Katrina.

It rains diamonds on Neptune, but have you
heard of black people not being around
where there's diamonds? We both form

from the pressure. Couldn't fill people
in Flint full of lead fast enough
so they just put it in the water.
Michigan is awful funny way to spell

Mississippi. You got a Jackson,
we got a Jackson. Ours just full
of inmates. No wonder
Hell is here. You didn't know

racists were up north
because you haven't been listening. Our

governor got an artificial
spine, he needs to repair
himself but Black don't crack,

we're basically immortal. The only thing
killing us is you. Kwame got thirty years,
but last time I checked he didn't poison
anybody. Let yal tell it, that's justice.

Yal be a plague, it's no wonder
yal call it germinating but
the Germans don't even support

Nazis like yal do. Detroit is coming back,
for the white supremacists who are

probably from, I don't know, Pluto. Small,
always overcompensating for something,
always far away from that which shines
too brightly, like the sun, like us.

The Plague

Black people don't have fears,
they have mamas, and ghosts,
finding out you're out
of coco butter and text me

when you get home. Deep down
everyone fears something,

keeps us from swan diving
into the abyss, going off
the last ledge we face

before hitting the water
our ancestors drowned
in. Once, I thought
I conquered my fears,

until getting my dad's bipolar,
stuck in this mental straitjacket,

always paranoid with myself.
Difficult determining the difference
between irrational terrors and threats,

cars backfiring or gunshots,
secretly my own being
terrifies me. I can't call
the police in peace, petrified
and panicking they'll have me
resting in peace, in pieces
from their lead pellets.

Gone are times when I could travel
through the wrong hood without
wondering if shots ring out from

the clan or my fellow black man.
Dream vacations turn nightmares
of me sold into the sex trade.

I am in a constant state of terror
and what's worse is I'm facing
my worst fears everyday. Being

someone's secret,
broken wedding vows,

being someone's ghost,
haunting them,
from the time
someone tried
to penetrate me
from the closet
he was hiding in
to now, the fact

that he's in prison
and doesn't know
doesn't make me feel
any better about lying
with her. I long to be loved

openly, claimed, not
someones hidden affair,
halfway across the country.

I ache for it, bedside beside a love,
which is mine. Even my ex, the witch
who I was engaged to, kept me hidden
for years. My mom appeases my concerns
with not my fault talk but I know this

as I do my inherited illness, as I do
that last time the cops keep capping
my corpse, as I do the specters
that haunt this body, that this

abyss is mine. I face it everyday.
It is a fate, worse than death,
to become what you fear.

Mental Straitjacket

The demons are circling,
closing in with their
Tiki torches and protests
for confederate flags,

and I'm not surprised. These devils
I've seen before with pitchforks, lynchings, dogs

and hoses and I've survived it all, but this illness
in my brain lies in wait with more intensity than any
clan can. It's funny how depression and white power

want the same destiny for me. There isn't a known
cure for either one, but I've dedicated my whole life
as a warlock searching books for a counter spell
to this curse. Depressed monkeys on my back,

the sight of you brings a smile
to my face. A simple

hello turns me into the center
of the universe. I know this
seems weird but I like you,

a lot and the clouds shrouding
my sunny days are gone when I see you.

I see the next fifty years of us
in your face. The medicated lobotomy
disappears and I become a mausoleum,
willing to share all of our skeletons,

all of our secrets together. All I want
is a love that makes me feel innocent,
again, like a naive little boy. A wizard

wishing he could will away
the haunting words of the clan,

and the alt-right, but my black magic isn't enough
without your love. The sound of your voice is what
my whole existence has led up to. Enslaved

on a slave ship, carried a cross across
my branded backside in past generations,all for this. The feeling of
your hands on my scalp

birthed thousands of stars in my chest. My spells
when well cast last lifetimes, and I know I'm appearing
like a strange deranged man but with all the hate I face

I just want to take a shot of love. You can't heal me of this
ailment, not alone at least, and I'm aware of this,
but my depression becomes a figment of my imagination
around you. I just want to sing your praises, reanimate

the dead and dance every time I think of you.
I know I've only known you for a short time,
but I can confidently say I love you,

for the very first time, I'm in love with the man
in the mirror the face, looking back at me
and it feels so refreshing to admit that.

Mausoleum

Teachers

I.

days spent
with captive
lizards, when
they went away

you know you shouldn't
have given black kids
something to love

all for you to take it
away. this was our
first lesson, but
I had already known,

been taught by
my father

(which many
of my classmates
didn't have the privilege
of having). I knew

how that which we love
leaves us, to be

       tested on
            or killed
in someone's laboratory

as if they didn't own
their own flesh
and bones, and many

years later, sitting
on that college

campus I wondered
what rooms our pet
iguana spent his

final moments in
and which ones
were innocent

Science/Eulogy to Puff Daddy

II.

Sorry. With
one comment

undoing
entire
lesson.

All because.
Sleeping.

the others in class
didn't know or care
about hearing
while still hibernating.

Words.
Weight.
Heavy.
Cost.

But I can not tell you
thanks today because of it.

English/Distraction

III.

first time
falling
asleep,
buckling
to nightmares

in your classroom,
the lesson,
compassion

for your fellow
human, when
seeing you
many years
later, shocked
to learn that I
am a teacher

I am surprised,
since you planted
the seeds all along

Language Arts/What We Grow Into

IV.

mathematics.
two feuding
students, shove
them in a car

with a gun
pointed
their way
blanketed
by your cries

for help.
recipe

for squashed beef.

when returning
to the track, not
best of friends
but the equation
checked out when
showing our work

Mathematics/Recipe for Squashed Beef

V.

small.
delicate

in my hands,
the gentle touch
of this frail
scared rodent.

while the others
focused on fear,
you took it. told
me to attempt

to draw it
or paint it,
knowing

art was not
one of my talents.
yet here I am,
an artist, and you
could see that
all along

from the way
catching it
came to me
and I didn't
even squeeze

Art/Catching the Mouse

VI.

secretary,
although

never secured
funds for
finding
ways to do
what we

wanted. still
this job,
you advised me

to take, my duty to serve
the entire student body.

learned about
accountability,
and negotiations,
and democracy,
and how most
won't appreciate

powers they wield
until it's too late
to fight back for
them. and I think

your most
important
lesson was
on revolution,
how it rarely
comes peacefully.

Government/Class Elections

VII.

targets

on my back,
shots fired.

Intelligent ones,
always first
to go. Especially
if they're black. you

taught me that.
wondering,

why you were gone
the next year,
thinking, you might
have worn the same
targets accidentally

branded on me
the day you said
I had a future

Social Studies/Targets

VIII.

turning on the lights,
paying on your car
or rent where you live,

choices you have
to make. when

going into the classroom,
smiles. laughs. when
leaving sorrow drowns you,
poverty strangles your neck,

suffocates you, as you go
through all of it over
again, you wonder

if this is what it was like
for all of your old teachers

Teachers

IX.

teaching

college classes,
one of the topics

good and bad
role models.
student names
someone. turning

to write it on the board
and another student asks
what they did. replies,

drugs.

to which it's stated
they do drugs now,
you gonna judge me?

this is my life now,
talking about drug use
with my students,

hilarity ensues,
because who said
you can't have laughter
in the classroom. They

turn to me to ask
questions
and with a smile
on my face, I answer

My Other Job

So, I'm standing here,
Dick, in my hand,
at my most vulnerable
After finishing masterbating

And there's blood, again.
My mom says it might
Be my prostate

My urges say rub it out again,
There might not be blood this time
it is, and I try again, and it is

My depression says at least it's at your own hand,
my poems say at least this death is at your own hand,
not by cop or rogue shooter

My medicine says we'll help with the depression.
My anxiety says oh shit.
nobody says save me,
I am not 30 yet

Maybe I'm just ripe enough, the blacker the berry,
the sweeter the juice,
my berry is so black
I can't ever get another job

with my name black. Maybe I am old enough,
maybe I am young enough,
maybe I'm lonely enough,

my loneliness says eat alone again. My loneliness says
invite nobody over. My loneliness says fade away
My big sis Legacy, says nothing
My big bro Blair, says nothing
My auntie Giselle says nothing

Death, the void that swallowed them
Says nothing, just smiles

My cat says meow, which translates to, I love you.
But he is not another human, who's touch I crave

My dreads say, nigga we just got here
My tinder profile doesn't know,My booking agent, doesn't know,

they are
For the future

I say, this poem,
I say, we got more work to do

I say,

I'm just standing here
With my meat out
Just finished masterbating

And there, is
No more blood,
No more left
To give

Blood

Chronology

sometimes hiding/
under blankets/

relieves me of stress/
and it always has/since

I was a child/afraid
of the world/outside/

and look at that/

it still does/

20 years later/

Poem Texted to Myself in the Bed

At times, I think about
what puny gods are we/

for the ants/and the flies/
who don't live/that long/

in our eyes/flies live about/
one months time/and I wonder/

how many of those prayers/did
I answer/ants live about 15 years/

and how many ants/have I seen/
in my lifetime/squashed or let live/

their whole existence/gone/and I
would barely notice/my cat is a creature/

of myth to these/tiny organisms/living
for 20 years/and how his prayers/take

priority/to me/he meows for food/or water/
or attention/and I answer/maybe even stepping/

on ants to do so/for a thing/that lives a quarter/
of my lifespan/and I get to thinking/what of our/

god/how do they answer our/tiny prayers/avoiding
stepping on us/how long do they/stay alive for/or
are they already dead/reborn/through these tiny

creatures.

Tiny Prayers

Even eroding/my teeth
away/will not divorce/

me from my love/of fruit
gushers/bringing back

times/when I was young-/
er and more innocent/times

when I could believe/in any-
thing/like that I was gonna be/

tall or that the future/bright
as can be/or even my belief/

in some guy/in the sky/watch-
ing over/my actions/causing

guilt/

Gushers

when the mind
attempts to under-

stand itself, it tries
to destroy itself,

and I think of this
fact, while scrolling

through my music
collection, after

Chris Cornell
took his own

life a year ago,
after Avicii

took his own life
6 months ago, all

my favorite artist
are committing

suicide and I wonder
does that mean they

understood them-
selves to the great-

est degree that
they could

Soundtrack

sometimes when listening to music,
escaping into my own head, back

there, terrified, wondering
if my next day will be my last,

talking to the fellow patients,
playing cards until someone,

asks me a question, and I snap
out of it. I'm in a car on the way

to a poetry slam in another city,
year and a half removed from

my time inside the hospital.
Sometimes, I'm not convinced

that I'm here until I'm doing
something I couldn't be in

there, like taking care of my cat
or attending poetry readings.

Sometimes, I think I'm still stuck
in the prison of the mind, going

back inside, it's just, matter of time
until I'm snapped out of it, by living

in the now, not in my past, not in
reliving moments of the past.

Having escaped, I put my headphones
back on my head, listening to music

until

Prison of the Mind

About narcolepsy,
you're always dreaming
even when you're not,

living out alternate realities
all the time, when sleeping
and awake tend to blend

together. I dreamed once,
I was holding hands with
your mother and we were
so happy about your coming

arrival. Dreamed of holding hands,
with you and your mother, waking
in the hospital, after a tragic heartbreak.

I don't even know what's real anymore,
sometimes I repeat phrases to make sure
I'm living in the now, but even that

about narcolepsy, always dreaming
when not, living out alternate realities.

I think I'm awake because I've got a hot
date with a woman, who's kiss reminds me
of little chocolates and my grandmother

and I can remember her hands. So soft
in my palms as I held them together,
it brought me back to a time when I thought
love could heal me of my narcolepsy

the thing about narcolepsy, you're always
dreaming even when you're not and hold on

did I already say that, already talk about
dreaming about us one time, about our kids,
and did I mention I rarely dream except

when I'm in love. I woke up this morning
and you were on my mind so I sent you
texts about our date later on tonight because

the space where I sleep is only shared with
those who are special to me, can help me,
snap out of it, and it's been occupied by
this cat too long. Essentially what I'm saying is

the thing about narcolepsy you're always
dreaming, even when you're not, living

out alternate realities and something
seems oddly familiar about you. I think
I dreamed up this moment of us meeting
one time before, or many times before

when we were just young and hopeful.
I guess what I'm saying is I can see into
thousands of tomorrows and I don't see

one I want to spend without your love
so I hope everything goes well with us

tonight because I don't want to wake up
in some strange ass hospital again heart
broken because the thing about narcolepsy
is you're always dreaming, even when

Alternate Realities

birth certificates,
in the safe
with the guns,

with my slave name

diplomas, my broken
laptop from years back,

notebooks containing years
of old love poems
that I used to write,

mail from over
many months
ago, innocence
and other falsehoods,

my sister, and her kids,
old photos of childlike
versions of me, my old

sneakers, televisions
and video games
from times long ago,

bags of clothes
not worn anymore,
my cats old food
and water bowls,

the engagement ring,
given to my ex that
gave him to me,

somewhere
hidden under
the bed

Things Left at 18063 Woodingham
after Francine Harris

the first person I met/
while dating online/

has gone missing/
and I have no means/
to contact her family/

one night/of passion/
ate lovemaking/which

fast forward through/
time/I wonder if it/

could be handled/different
-ly/remembering her stretch/

marks in my hands/thinking
we'd see each other/again/

but after/that one night/she
has disappeared/with no trace/

for me to find/her, even her phone/
now shut off/and when we last spoke/

she was worried/about where/she was/
going to stay/besides/my memories/

What Happened at 15791 Cherrylawn

"first they came for the communists, and I did not speak out"
                                    - Martin Niemoller

wrongly attributed quote
about caring about
someone else, not

giving damns until
they came for you

but I didn't think about
that until I was held by
the law for having
suspended license

but what would I know
from here with smudged
glasses sitting on the outside

now, surely I wouldn't have
learned from that lesson

Smudged Glasses

during late nights, speaking
to my cat, swearing he
understands me, when
she was alive, my great
grandmother called my
father a good for nothing
nigga, not knowing what
he would suffer through
after the stroke, or maybe
she did, able to see that
far into the future, linear
time escapes me now
and I think of her last
moments, how she resigned
and almost accepted her fate,
how that might be my future
and I tell my cat all of this

and he just meows, before
looking out the window,
gazing into some far away
land that I cannot see, and

essentially what I'm asking
is about how it's a strange
kind of witchcraft when our

family lives on in the animals
we leave behind on this earth

Strange Witchcraft

black cat/chat noir/
whatever you call/

him, me and my pet/
live in this world/away/

from all my illnesses/
         anxiety/   depression/   bipolar/   narcolepsy/

we live in these/ moments/
of peace/and isn't that too/

a blessing/to live in this/
world of stress/and find/

delight/in your being/a man
and his cat/I ate today/and

that too is something/to be
grateful for/and I am/thankful/

to be alive/to live out/all/
these/moments/these/these alternate/   time lines/

with my little buddy/beside me/

Hanging in There

wake up/shower/
get dressed/call

an uber/tell story/

BOMBS EXPLODE

go to bed/repeat/wake
up/shower/get dressed/

GUN FIRE NONSTOP

call an uber/tell story/
go to bed/repeat/wake up/

shower/get dressed/call

ARRESTED,INCARCERATED

an uber/tell story/go to bed/repeat/
wake up/

every/time/I wake/up/and tell/
the story/about how I used to be/
just/like them/to another uber/
driver until/my ex broke up with/

ME/

another day/goes by/and I get/
to shower/get dressed/and live/
out my day/as if/millions/aren't

DYING

every day/in corners/of the world/
unable to imagine/been couple/of

days/and I forgot/to shower/to break

THE CYCLE

for a little bit/and think about/their
lives/repeat/repeat/repeat/repeat/

Wake up/shower/get dressed/
call an uber/tell story/go to bed/   repeat

The Cycle

Mike brown died/
because of mistaken/

identity at a gas station/
and Trayvon Martin/

did the same thing/
getting skittles

and iced tea/both
mistaken for monsters/

and while the pumps/
burn/they're memory

lives on as beasts/
in the minds/of these

white people/afraid
of the unknown

       un-owned
            what they

don't understand

Mistaken For Monsters

plumbers come over to fix
my bathtub, drain clogged
with too much hair, again.

this only happens after
the winter has ended
and I again become
human. My doctor

prescribed me vitamin D
pills, says I need to get
more sunlight. Normally

devoured whole, without
water, this is how I consume

most of my meals, when
getting to have them. Women
come over and never return

time and time again. I feat my
werewolf blood manifests but
remembering if I just made that
up, as a figment of imagination

or explanation for my sexual
appetite is unclear. What I do

know is that I silently hunger
so much that I produced blood
while rubbing it out into the toilet

an embarrassment I had to conceal
from all others for as long as possible.

Lycanthrope

If able, to take back/
this numbness, in my/

toes, for a moment/
I would cherish the/

feeling of gravel/
and grass under/

my feet/the distinct/
ability to feel things/

with my toes/now
my cat licks them/
and I barely feel/a thing/

Feet

Ok, so this is gonna be difficult/
11:15am, August 12, 2018/

attempting to speak/to my past/
self/so let's see how it goes/

how are you?/
comment ca va?/

good/bien/
how old are you/

quel âge avez-vous?/
I am twenty nine/

J'ai treize ans/
Parlez-vous toujours français/

No but I am relearning French/
It's so amazing to speak to you/

Oui/Quel est l'avenir comme/
well/I can't tell you that/might

alter my timeline/but I can tell you/
you are a poet now/un poete?/I know

it's a long and complicated story/Your
favorite colors are still/rouge, noir/yes

red and black/you own a black cat now/
chat noir?/yep, you do/he's so cute/

est-ce que je trouve l'amour/no, no, we're
still looking for that/it's actually how we

became a poet

Conversation With My Past Self

Buried beneath our basement
you found three
African dolls
father, mother
and child
before you even knew
they would become
the future for you

African Dolls

They called me hyper/
even though/sleeping
all the time/in every

class./I didn't know/

what I was honestly/
just knowing/I didn't

belong./Can one not/
be himself/if he has
never loved?/I mean,

if everything/is a secret/
do those ever come out?/

Having loved many women/
I know what/being welcome/
is supposed to feel like/and

I've felt home/in more women/
than I can name/but when he

smacked/my ass, I kinda liked it,/
I just didn't know/he would try/
to come by and rape me/later
that night/while I slept/like

class/a helpless student./

Lessons

Nobody else
to blame
your first
engagement failed

because of you.
Call a spade
a spade

and you find one
in your mirror

digging you deeper
in your grave
of guilt. Some friends

aren't friends
anymore
because of it
and there is no credit

to go anywhere else.
And your fiancee looks
at you with eyes

full of forgiveness
something you have never

experienced before
and you want to cry
there are so many

graves of past loves
who died for me
to come to this
and I am so sorry

and she just holds
you, says

it will all be alright

and for once
you believe it.

Blame

My ex, a stepping stool
to what is now, this

heaven, built from
the hell she caused,

climbing on her back,
after the destruction.

Forgive me, for ever
loving others before

you. Their calamity
looked so enticing.

Letting others love
you before you met

me, forgive me. Your
prayers, lost to space

and time. And time
heals all wounds

but I can't have it
back. All loves

before you were
ladders, climbed

so I could get to
you. Sorry. Desole.

Armageddons, faced
and resurrected, many

times, until getting
to the treasure that

is your heart. Los
siento. When
looking there are
constellations

dedicated to your
body, the mother
of our children.

Calamity

Acknowledgments

The author thanks, appreciates and acknowledges the following publications in which poems from this collection previously appeared:

82 Review: "Whale"

Blacktop Passages: "Strange Witchcraft"

Gyroscope Review: "Teachers"

Mobius: The Journal For Social Change: "Mausoleum", "Casualties", "Lycanthrope"

One Sentence Poems: "Awkward", "Expendable", "Microaggressions", "Black Love", "Things Left at 18063 Woodingham"

Panoplyzine: "November Nights"

Quiet Storm: "Prison of the Mind"

Rising Phoenix Press: "Old Times", "Lazarus"

Rogue Agent Journal: "4 East"

Vitamin ZZZ: "Poem I Texted to Myself in the Bed", "Hanging in There", "Alternate Realities"

Wayne Literary Review: "Teachers", "Connection", "Death by Cop", "Skin Doesn't Know Your Touch"

Wild Age Press: "Post Credit Scene: Fireworks"

Z Publishing, Michigan's Best Emerging Poets: "Eternal Sunshine of the Spotless Mind"

About the Author

Deonte Osayande is a writer from Detroit, MI. His books include *Class* (Urban Farmhouse Press, 2017) and *Circus* (Brick Mantle Books, 2018). His nonfiction and poetry have been nominated for the Best of the Net Anthology, and the Pushcart Prize. He has represented Detroit at four National Poetry Slam competitions. He's currently a professor of English at Wayne County Community College. He also managed the Rustbelt Midwest Regional Poetry Slam and Festival for 2014 and 2018.

CPSIA information can be obtained
at www.ICGtesting.com
Printed in the USA
FFHW021956101019
55481672-61277FF